Why Are They Like That?
Men

*Questions you've dared to ask, answered
by real people, celebrities and experts*

A book series based on the award-winning
sharing project that's captured worldwide
attention helping people in their personal,
social and business relationships

Phillip J. Milano

For Robin, Jacob, Lucas and Ben

Publisher:
Y Forum
yforum@yforum.com

ISBN: 978-1-07-954123-6

Cover and interior layout by Sandy Weber,
Key 3 Creative, Jacksonville, Florida
Cover photo credit: Rawpixel. Stock photo for illustrative purposes
only; any person depicted is a posed model.

Content based in part on the popular Y? sharing project and Dare
to Ask column

Find out more about the author, upcoming books and speeches at
www.phillipmilano.com, www.facebook.com/PhillipJMilano or
@PhillipMilano.

Books In This Series

Why Are They Like That? Blacks

Why Are They Like That? Whites

Why Are They Like That? Hispanics

Why Are They Like That? Asians

Why Are They Like That? Gay Men

Why Are They Like That? Lesbians

Why Are They Like That? Women

Why Are They Like That? Men

Why Are They Like That? Rich and Poor

Why Are They Like That? Religious (or not)

Why Are They Like That? Disabled People

Why Are They Like That? Young and Old

Praise for the Y? sharing project and the book "I Can't Believe You Asked That!" (Perigee)

"Milano is quietly revolutionizing cross-cultural communication..."
- Pulitzer Prize-winning columnist Leonard Pitts

"If you've ever hesitated to ask a question because you think it might be considered insensitive or impolitic, now is your chance ... Nothing is considered out of bounds..."
- CNN Headline News

"(It) tells more about who we are and how we feel about each other than you're likely to learn from a dozen sociology texts…"
- Washington Post News Service

"Mr. Milano has dared to open the field of debate to the maximum…"
- Le Monde, Paris

"(A) remarkable contribution to cross-cultural understanding…"
- The (London) Guardian

"A truly rare achievement … has the potential to have a profound impact on the way we all see and understand each other..."
- Playboy magazine

"It's an incredible book. It diffuses everything ... Nothing is off limits, and the questions have that childlike honesty to them..."
- Dee Snider, Twisted Sister; host, "Dee Snider Radio"

"A take-no-prisoners attitude prevails between the volume's covers . . . This book is hard to put down..."
- Midwest Book Review

"A+ (highest rating) … Everything you wanted to know but were afraid to ask gets tackled here ..."
- Entertainment Weekly

CONTENTS

Introduction

Why Are They Like That? is a series of books based on an award-winning worldwide sharing project in which real people, experts and celebrities talk about things that make us different from each other. Silly things. Sad things. Funny things. Profound things.

Read with an open mind and we believe that by the time you're finished you'll have a much better understanding of how to make more and real friends, money and love. It's that simple.

Why? Because this isn't about trying to get ahead with diversity training. We are well beyond that. According to the Census Bureau, by 2050 the United States will have no racial or ethnic minority.

No, this is about moving past talking about how to understand each other to talking to each other. Right now.

That's why there's no agenda to these books other than getting the conversation going. We can discuss studies and methods for elevating social consciousness all we want, but there is no substitute for real dialogue.

That's where Why Are They Like That? stands apart from other books on the topic. You will see how people talk about their real differences of race, religion, sex, disability and more.

The success of the approach is proven: It's based on the ground-breaking Y? website project, blog and column that have attracted millions of visitors and worldwide media attention.

Our hope is that by reading, you will become more comfortable asking and answering the questions yourself, expecting the unexpected in return and helping change the ground rules for how we learn from and about each other. To that end, we wrap up each book in the series with our O.U.T.L.O.U.D. Method for Dialogue, with tips to help you get your own conversations started. Ultimately, that is what this effort is all about.

After all, if you want to make more friends, money and love, you better know the people you're talking to, selling to or opening up to. Knowledge isn't just power. It's all power.

Enjoy.

Phillip J. Milano
Founder, Y?

Hey rude boy! Open the door, willya?

They asked:

Why is it so hard to find men between 22 and 33 who are old-fashioned? Decently dressed, well-kept, good taste, open doors...

Cynthia, 25, Toronto, Canada

You said:

Respect for other people is being slowly bred out of our culture.

M., 39, male, Hickory, N.C.

A lot of women (myself included) ... feel men like this think we are fragile. Apparently, men picked up on this. Good for them.

Ember, Phoenix

Asking a guy in his 20s to have good taste? They're college sophomores — the origin of the term "sophomoric humor."

Chris, 51, male, Windsor, Conn.

If I'm at a party with the bad-boy player, I won't get a second glance. You are looking right through us.

Ralph, 34, New Jersey

With equal rights, men questioned women's desire for this treatment.

Charles, Detroit

If a boy's father wasn't like that, he won't be.

Bethany, 17, Medford, Ore.

It's usually the not-so-attractive guys who are the nicest, because they have to make up for the lack of looks. Maybe you're looking in the wrong places.

Nick, 23, Newburgh, Ind.

Men aren't taught to respect women (with porn easily available) [and] women 18-27 like to be treated like shit and pieces of meat.

Q., 25, male, Seattle

Everyone — man, woman or hermaphrodite — needs good manners.

Julie, 33, Woodbridge, Va.

We found:

About 30 percent of men practice it. Another 40 percent want it. The rest just don't get it.

Proper etiquette, that is.

So says Valerie Peterson-Kelly, founder of Houston-based A Very Positive Outlook (verypositiveoutlook.com), a fatherhood consultant that teaches men manners.

"It's still pretty bad out there. It's across the board," said Peterson-Kelly, author of the kids book "Where's My Daddy?" "Men who wear suits, the etiquette piece goes out the door once they're out of the spotlight. And blue-collar guys? They're like 'What the hell, I'm going to get my TV tray, and I don't give a rip what people say, I'm going to do my thing.' "

The main problem is men aren't around enough, especially at dinner time, she said. It's one thing for Mom to talk about manners; it's another to have a male role model get the boys' attention when giving instructions.

"No male is saying 'Stop all that burping, scratching and farting at the dinner table' or 'How would you like your daughter bringing that home?' "

The No. 1 thing not being taught boys: courting.

"No one's telling a young man how to act or talk on a date, that a girl shouldn't be called a 'B' or 'H' or 'skank.' It's all about selfish tendencies now," Peterson said. "No 'ladies first.' There's no sacrifice."

Should he search long and wide for a new partner?

They asked:

My fiancee told me shortly before our wedding that I was not the "man" who could fulfill her. Our sex life now suffers. I've read books, got advice from friends, sought help ... and all have done nothing. I know if I feel like a man I'll treat her like one. But how? Will only a $30,000 to $50,000 surgery fix the problem?

Jim, 26, Boulder, Colo.

You said:

This seems like the beginning of the end, homie.

Jim, 30, Columbus, Ohio

A better question is why a loving, creative partner isn't enough. Have you ever thought maybe it isn't you?

Merry, 41, Atlanta

You not only listen to her, you take total blame for this "problem" and try everything to please her. These are not the actions of an immature individual or frat boy; this is a man taking action. This shouldn't make you feel stupid or ashamed. Every couple has trouble adjusting to a new life together. Have you asked her what, exactly, she wants? If that doesn't work, try a professional.

Katie, Lexington, Ky.

Confidence is everything.

Bethany, 24, Michigan

Dump that bitch and find a woman you can satisfy.

Kofi, Jersey City, N.J.

You said once you feel like a man you'll treat her like one. Does that mean you'd likely punch her and make her do dishes? Preferably not. ... Being comfortable to be yourself — that's a true man.

Steven, 25, Houston

10

You deserve better.

Kelly, 27, Houston

We found:

We don't have much space, so we'll conveniently skip the "how-to" advice and the surgery stuff, thank you very much, and focus on the how-in-creation-could-things-get-to-this-point part.

"Somebody decides they need something they don't have, but they avoid talking about it," said Suzanna Hillegass (shillegass.com), a Virginia relationship therapist. "But in this case, it's like me saying to my hubby, 'I want you to be 6 inches taller.' It doesn't compute."

Instead of trying to change someone, discuss how you can get more of a need fulfilled — and in this case, that means talking about stimulation, she said.

"It's not rocket science."

If the problem is left to fester, then the man's hurt will lead him to think there's something fundamentally wrong with himself, and he'll withdraw physically, Hillegass said.

"And in our culture everything is ... driven to a quick fix. Instead it should be something we talk about, work through. It's a great opportunity they're missing."

Her advice to this couple is to realize that being intimate is multi-faceted and is about having a "more whole experience," she said.

"But he also needs to pay attention. This may not be a match made in heaven. Can they take this on as a challenge that he wants to satisfy her, and that she needs to learn to be satisfied with him how he is? Is she willing to work on this with him?"

That'd be a labor of love.

11

They came, they saw ... they hit on them

They asked:

Some of my teenage female students tell me they are hit on so much by men, all ages, all ethnicities, that they are afraid to go buy gas alone. These aren't skanky girls. What gives?

T.R., 48, female, Jacksonville

You said:

The media, advertising and our general culture teaches men that all women are available (for the right price). Men are told that "no" means "yes" and that any woman who bothers to put on lipstick is actively trolling for sex with anyone who happens to want her. I've heard a guy say that any woman who works out to have a good figure must be a slut.

D.L., female, Los Angeles

I'm so sick of men's demeaning catcalls and staring at me like a piece of meat. It makes me wary of all men because it has happened so often. It seems to be a way for them to gain control of us. It's harassment, but since it happens so often in the public setting, people have resorted to "ignoring" it instead of doing something about it.

Mariam, 19, Bay Area, Calif.

Nowadays you can't even tell a woman they look beautiful or any kind of compliment without them feeling you are attempting to win them over for some other agenda. I know all about harassment. I worked at a bar for more than a year where 90 percent of our private parties were older women, and they would harass me and another bartender constantly. I don't like hearing guys whistle or yell down the street at women they don't know. It's childish and ignorant, but nowadays a lot of younger women seem to enjoy it.

Rick, 27, Trenton, N.J.

We found:

It's a low-down "dirty old man" fact that dudes have always been horny.

Males of all species are easily aroused sexually and are inclined to look for extra partners, said David P. Barash (dpbarash.com), professor of psychology at the University of Washington and co-author of "The Myth of Monogamy" and "Strange Bedfellows."

"The best strategy evolutionary-wise is to be fast and loose," said Barash, who researches evolutionary biology. "It's because those who are more successful produce more offspring."

Even if a guy isn't looking to procreate, natural selection has endowed him with a "sexual sweet tooth" — a penchant for responding to reproductive needs with sexual arousal.

Research shows that young women can be more attractive to, say, a middle-aged man because women who are similar in age to the older man have likely gone through menopause — and that means they've lost at least some of their sexual attractiveness, Barash said.

"Women who are age 18 to 30 are the most attractive, which is when they are also the most reproductive."

The bottom line is men have a lower threshold when it comes to showing sexual interest, he said.

"Studies show that a woman will smile, and the guy thinks, 'She's coming on to me,' while the woman just feels she's being nice, and has no sexual interest in him at all."

Nice guys finish in the back seat?

They asked:

Why do girls always think guys are only out for sex? For example, when a guy acts nice to so many girls, they claim he wants to get in their pants. When did it become a crime to just be nice?

Robert, 17, Cromwell, Conn.

You said:

Maybe you should listen to your fellow men sometimes. Which is more common: "I'd jump on that!" or "I bet she's really sweet"? Which would most guys go to first, a strip club or a coffee shop? Hooters or Buffalo's? As the old saying goes, "Guys use love to get sex and women use sex to get love."

Mara D., Dallas, Ga.

It's a defense mechanism because they've probably been hit on since they were like 15 by any number of dudes from different age ranges. And all of them were being "nice" to her.

Jacob H., Atlanta

Unfortunately, when a female thinks a male is only out for sex, it is a barrier she places between herself and them, based on past experiences or the neglect of a "good" man in her life. Therefore, she views men as "dogs" and their very purpose is to get some.

Lyrick, 20, female, Washington, D.C.

When women . . . have guys "talk" to their [breasts] instead of looking them in the eyes, it's not hard to see why many think guys are only out for sex.

Shelly, 49, Pennsylvania

Some guys really are out for nothing but sex, and more have sex as a definite goal than are generally willing to admit it. On the other hand, ladies, there is a point at which it should become clear whether sex is the guy's primary goal or not.

Jason, Bloomington, Ind.

We found:

Is it true that ever since the first man grunted empathetically to a woman or rolled a cave door open for her that he was really just trying to get under her bison hide?

To hear L.A. dating coach Evan Marc Katz (evanmarckatz.com) talk about the present-day love game, you'd have to say it's quite possible.

"Generally women have it right . . . often a guy is trying to get to know a woman under the guise of friendship so he can get close to her to ask her out," said Katz, who focuses on helping women understand men and is the author of the book "Why You're Still Single."

"This guy [Robert, above] … sounds in denial. What does he want, a new friend? Most women know better."

Above all, Katz says, women want men who don't kowtow.

"Most men in healthy relationships treat their women well. But also, men have balls and they make decisions. Nice guys try to 'nice' their way into women's hearts. If there's a crime in being 'nice,' it's that it's ineffective [to getting a date]. She wants a man she will respect and look up to. She doesn't need a valet — 'Oh can I get your bags for you?' etc.

"There's nothing wrong with being nice . . . it's when you put a woman on a pedestal that things don't work if you're trying to date her."

And if Robert really is just trying to be nice?

"He has nothing to worry about. The only reason he has to worry is if he is using friendship as a way to ask her out and it's not working."

Stay on your side of the bed ... son?

They asked:

My ex-wife continues to sleep with our 10-year-old son when he stays at her house. This is not a sexual thing. Is this unusual?

Joe, 51, Florida

You said:

I would be worried. Ten-year-old boys are coming into their sexual maturity soon, and they don't need to wake up with their mom lying next to them.

Sheri, 41, San Francisco

Your ex-wife is forming a closer bond. The mother has the power to impact her child for life. Your ex-wife feels it's not wrong to sleep with her 10-year-old son as long as the tie produces a healthy relationship. I concur.

L.C., Greenville, Miss.

She's way over-attached, and it might not be overtly sexual, but there's a serious "ick" factor, which will only get ickier as your son gets closer to puberty.

A., female, Missouri

If you're sure it's not in a sexual way, and the child is developing in a "normal" manner (he's not acting out sexually, he's developing appropriate boundaries, etc.), and she's not exposing him to her sexual activity, I'd say you're overreacting. There are cultures where the communal bed is kept for the entire life of a child.

Shelly, 49, New Alexandria, Pa.

We found:

As with most issues, there are two sides to this mattress. Developmental psychologist Aletha Solter (awareparenting.com), founder of The Aware Parenting Institute and author of "Helping Young Children Flourish," tucks in on the softer side, so to speak.

"It is normal for children to want closeness and reassurance at night whenever there is stress in their lives, because stress increases a child's attachment needs. Divorce of the parents can be a very stressful experience for children," she said.

"Many children feel that their family has fallen apart, and they often blame themselves or fear that their parents will stop loving them. If [the] son is unable to sleep alone because of chronic anxiety, it might be a good idea for him to see a competent psychotherapist."

Not to throw rocks in that bed, but Kevin Kennedy, senior child psychologist with Harvard Vanguard Medical Associates in Boston, says, uh-uh.

Occasional visits to the parents' bed at scary times are OK, but overall (in U.S. culture at least), "It's not a good idea in terms of promoting autonomy. Kids should gain independence and ability to do things by themselves, like sleeping."

In divorces, where the child may seek increased closeness, Kennedy suggests running errands or completing projects together more often.

"Sometimes divorced parents respond in terms of their own need of companionship. It's [sleeping together] done under the guise of sensitivity to the child, but the parents are really meeting their own needs."

And as a child gets older, things can get trickier.

"It's treacherous territory when kids are 10 or 11, in pre-adolescence, where erotic aspects can be a factor," he said. "I advise parents to never do it."

Are women pretty cheeky about men's butts?

They asked:

When a woman makes a comment about a guy's butt, what is she attracted to?

Peter, 33, Lehigh Valley, Pa.

You said:

Ah, these are the eternal mysteries.

Stephanie, 23, Norman, Okla.

It's probably the most attractive male body part, other than face and hands, for me.

L.K., 22, female, Laurel, Md.

My thinking is that it's a way in which women can "get back" at men for their remarks about our body parts. I do tend to look at the front side myself.

Cindy, 42, Venezuela

I can't say why a man's huge pecs and butt are so great to look at, but they are. Some women may not tell you this: A guy with a great body is a real head-turner.

Lynn, Lexington, Ky.

It's because they look good. And yes, I do think about squeezing them. But . . . a guy's butt is one of the last things I associate with sex. Hands and eyes are sexier.

Amber, Barrow, Alaska

It's definitely a turn-on, and on some level I am thinking about how it would feel if we were intimate. It's lovely to be able to run my hand down a man's back and reach something firm. And it adds to the sensation of being close to each other because I can pull him close with a body part of his that is firm and delightful to the touch. To add to this, a firm body is attractive. I like to feel a firm body next to mine, to feel the contours of a man's body. A great butt is a fine addition!

B.L., 22, Oakland, Calif.

We found:

We're writing about men's butts and we cannot lie.

And though we are secure in our manhood, let's stop the tinge of discomfort we feel right about now and cheekily quote someone else, some females, thank-you-very-much.

"One is a cultural answer: the buttocks have often been considered in many cultures to be highly related to sexual attraction," says Jennifer Bass (kinseyinstitute.org), spokeswoman for the Kinsey Institute for Research in Sex, Gender and Reproduction.

"Another is biological: evolutionary psychologists will talk about the shape [of the buttocks] and how it can represent a man's fertility. . . . It's the idea that they'll have some good genes, so it has to do with the kind of offspring you'll create."

And from a sexual perspective, "There's the idea that the buttocks are erotic areas, that touching them is arousing."

Heather Rupp, a cognitive neuroscientist and research fellow at Kinsey who has studied what women find attractive in men, said most females eye a man's face rather than his body.

However, women who are gauging men's masculinity (and therefore their testosterone levels for reproduction) may be attracted to males with more definitive muscles, she said.

"And remember, it's [the buttocks] a big ol' muscle, I think the biggest in the body. So they may be gauging the overall masculinity of a man by his buttocks."

They don't call it the gluteus maximus for nothing.

Is it a bald-faced lie that a combover is OK?

They asked:

Why do some men attempt to cover their balding heads with a comb-over? You all would look much more attractive if you would get a decent haircut. My gentleman friend reacted like I asked him to cut off his you-know-what when I suggested he would look much better if he changed his style.

Jo, 53, Fort Wayne, Ind.

You said:

We all want to look our best, and at our age most of us have come to the conclusion that "we can't please everybody, so we please ourselves." If you love him, don't ask him to change. If you don't love him, why should he change for you?

Carol S., 58, Mountain Home, Ark.

My hair loss is not yet severe, but I do find it disturbing. I think it engenders the opinion that anything on top of the head looks better than bare scalp.

Scott, 39, Bangor, Maine

Heh, the comb-over is apparently a hot look if you're Donald Trump. No one likes to be told what to do, especially if it concerns personal style. It's like why some women wear push-up bras that squish them into having cleavage with the aid of lots of wire and padding.

Ann, 22, Toronto

We found:

He may have mysteriously been elected leader of the still-free world, but we can trump the Donald as far as influentials who've sported this hairstyle. How about the ruler of most of the civilized world at one point?

That's right: Julius Caesar. He apparently had an exquisite combover, said Chris Marino. On statues you'll see that he pulled his hair way too far forward. He may even have worn that laurel to draw attention away from his eminent eggheaded-ness, Marino said.

Why are we quoting Chris Marino, anyway? Well, he spent two years making the documentary "Combover: The Movie" (79% on the Tomatometer at Rottentomatoes.com).

"We found that with most guys it starts out combing over a small patch of baldness . . . at some point, though, they lose touch with what's going on. Many are then in denial."

Marino said hair has always been an important symbol of virility and strength. While the comb-over style is fading and is mostly the province of older men, they will go to great lengths to advertise that they still have some fuzz left.

"We came across a gentleman in Texas who had one of the most incredible comb-overs I've ever seen. He was completely bald except for by his ears and back of his head. He grew that long enough so he could take it in three sections and . . . he could lap it in such a way it would cover every bit of scalp. Then he'd spray it down."

For those needing lessons, check out U.S. Patent 4,022,227 (complete with hand-illustrated diagrams), awarded in 1977 to Donald J. Smith and his father, Frank J. Smith, of Orlando. The elder Smith had big plans for wind-proof hair products and got a patent on a variation of the combover as the foundation of a future planned empire.

The tutorial may not be needed, though. A Psychology Today survey found only a minority of women find bald men unattractive.

If you can't do it, do you still think about it?

They asked:

If a man is medically impotent, as from diabetes, does he still have a sex drive?

Amy, 56, Jacksonville

You said:

Sexual excitement is a personal matter that can vary, but where there is a will there is a way! With a loving, caring partner, all kinds of good things can still happen. Intimacy in sexuality and a broader repertoire of activities can help. It depends on the degree of neuropathy as well. Diabetics often do not respond as well to drugs such as Viagra, etc., but they have very good response with the drug Caverject. It works with or without a strong libido.

Paul, 53, diabetic, Normal, Ill.

I've been on certain medications for some time that inhibit my sexual performance. But I still have a sex drive.

Bill, 43, Naples

Many times someone who has this type of condition will still have a sex drive; that is something that is biologically in you. Nerve damage and things like that do not seem to have a relation.

Saluki Girl, Carbondale, Ill.

I am a borderline (Type 2) diabetic. A man can certainly continue to some degree to have sexual desire and arousal and release. Unless something is really wrong psychologically, a man desires sex, virtually all the time.

Jerry, 58, Jacksonville

We found:

The endocrinological, psychological and societal implications of diabetes and other manifestations of impaired glucose metabolism in humans can impact regimens such as insulin therapies conducted to ameliorate the disorder and/or its inherent side effects.

OK, now that that's out of the way:

Why is Paul pushing this Caverject stuff, anyway? Does he realize where it's injected?

To get at the nut of this matter, we must first remember that the question is not about the heavy lifting, but wanting to do the heavy lifting.

And that desire is not affected by diabetes, says Robert Rizza, past president of the American Diabetes Association and professor of medicine at the Mayo Clinic in Minnesota (mayo.edu).

"Diabetes can affect a variety of things, but not libido," he said.

"It involves changes in blood flow in various parts of the body, and it can damage nerves and blood vessels and cause impotence."

To prevent the impotence, take care of the diabetes that's causing it, he added. That means healthful eating, exercise, blood glucose testing and possibly insulin therapy. An aspirin a day helps control blood vessels, Rizza said.

Who should care? About 10 percent of all U.S. males over age 20 (and their significant others, we guess). That's how many of them have diabetes, according to the American Diabetes Association. And of those, up to 75 percent will experience impotence because of it.

Why men don't like getting down to 'lady business'

They asked:

Why don't guys like to hear about our menstrual cycles?
Deborah K., 16, Richmond, Va.

You said:

I guess it is the same reason we don't want to hear about any of your other bodily functions. Men tend to idealize women, and we don't want to think of the less pleasant aspects of your physiology.
Cal, 43, Lakewood, Calif.

I have never experienced this shyness. I have never had a problem purchasing feminine products for girlfriends. This amazed my wife when we met. She had never encountered a guy who didn't mind going to the store for tampons and Midol.
Roger D., 33, Roanoke, Va.

Each sex has its own little foibles to deal with; those of the other sex seem gross and alien in comparison because we didn't grow up with those problems. That said, openly discussing bodily functions with someone not in the medical field is considered rude and disgusting.
Katie, Lexington, Ky.

We found:

It took us many minutes to find a guy willing to talk about this. He's curator of the more than 20-year-old Museum of Menstruation (www.mum.org), which he operated out of his home outside Washington until 1998, when it went exclusively online.

Harry Finley has lots to say about "Lady Business." His Web site, which has been praised by Kotex and which The New York Times says treats the topic in "an odd, funny and well-researched" manner, discusses how a woman's cycle has throughout history been perhaps the mother of all taboos, simply because so many see it as "unclean" or "unhealthy."

Finley finds the topic fascinating because it touches upon "medicine, anthropology, sociology, history and even art" — and because it's been handled so oddly: Some cultures segregated women in huts during their menstruation; women were accused of ruining crops or spoiling wine because they were in their cycle; ads dating back to 1928 heralded products to eliminate "offense to others;" and patent medicines in the late 19th century, such as Lydia Pinkham's Vegetable Compound, promised to cure "all those painful Complaints and Weaknesses so common to our best female population."

Even as late as 1992, Kotex ran a comic-strip style magazine ad that implied a girl might "change schools" if a boy she liked found out she was having her period.

As for men, Finley says the topic conflicts with their idealized view of the woman's body. As well, he said, it deals with female bodily functions, intimacy and emotions — a troika of topics many men don't care to discuss.

Also, when the subject does come up, women are usually complaining about it, Finley said. Nonetheless, we should listen and discuss it, he contends.

"It would be good if we did talk about it more, especially for women. It makes it more of a public, acceptable thing. You feel relieved when you know you're not alone.

"Now, I don't know if men will ever buy into that, but . . ."

Should he stop pounding the porn keys if she asks?

They asked:

To men: If you had a great sexual relationship, but your partner did not want you looking at porn because it bothered her, would you stop?

T.H., 20, female, S.C.

You said:

Are you crazy?

Carl, 30, Hamden, Conn.

I wouldn't. Men have porn, women have Cosmo.

Ethan, 32, New Orleans

My partner using porn makes me see him differently, as if there is a superficial part of his personality. I don't understand how such a sensitive man can pay himself and me so little respect.

Sharon, 29, United Kingdom

Porn is as important as personal hygiene. You could survive without it, but why would you want to?

Dorato, male, Kansas City, Mo.

I would give it up. But no more "Oooh, Brad Pitt is sooo sexy!" And tear down the Orlando Bloom posters. Fair is fair.

Glenn, 41, Canada

One powerful element is that he can see beautiful women doing anything, anytime, without limit. It's like Scrooge McDuck when he swims in his money.

Jack C., 45, Indianapolis

With a "great sexual relationship," why does your partner need pornos?

Jerry, 60, Marco Island

Men and women have used porn since the first Troglodyte carved a boo-boo doll out of a hunk of wood from the fire pit.

Mike, Grand Rapids, Mich.

He should respect your wishes and "cheat" no more.

Charlie, 34, Knoxville, Tenn.

Those not bitten by the porn bug should flee from it, as an obese person should avoid streets lined with bake shops.

Ronald V., 47, Canada

We found:

Gentlemen, start your search engines. Or, perhaps don't.

Raunch these days pretty much means cyber-raunch, and lots of men and women keep that dirty little secret, says Arizona physician Jennifer P. Schneider (jenniferschneider.com), co-author of "Cybersex Exposed: Simple Fantasy or Obsession?" and "Untangling the Web: Breaking Free From Sex, Porn, and Fantasy Obsession in the Internet Age."

The prurient . . . er, salient ... interest here is how often and why someone's doing it, and how much it bugs his mate, she said.

"Those are hours he could be with his wife and kids. On the other hand, if it's just entertainment, it may be a matter of negotiation. But if he is seeing stuff that leads him to make requests of his wife she's not comfortable with, that's a problem. It's not always about morality. Usually it's about the relationship."

Why do folks gawk to begin with? To generalize: For men, it's to quench visual fantasy needs and add naughty novelty to a routine sex life, Schneider said, and for women, it's about intimacy and relationships. That's why men hit the jpg and mpeg sites and women frequent adult chat rooms.

Research shows about 10 percent to 15 percent of people into cyberporn get flat-out compulsive about it. Of those, 30 percent of the men end up cheating with real live people; 70 percent of the women do the same. And that ain't idle chit-chat.

Do guys really need to hork one up in front of others?

They asked:

Why do men need to spit so much in public?

Anne, Jacksonville Beach

What is it with guys and spitting?

Cheryl, New Haven, Conn.

You said:

It's a macho thing, pure and simple.

Aloysius, 37, male, Atlanta

I, too, have noticed this a lot. Just yesterday I was stopped at a light and the man in front of me opened his door to let one go. I wish they would stop. Why can't they just use a restroom?

Amy, 29, Portland, Ore.

And there's always the danger of it hitting someone. I was walking out of school one day, and this guy suddenly spat to one side. I was standing right there and had to go the rest of the way home with it on my jacket. All the way I was thinking, ew, ew, ew.

H., 16, female, United Kingdom

Probably it is a subconscious urge to mark one's territory.

Augustine, 40, male, Columbia, S.C.

It's considered "unladylike" to hock a big loogie while walking down the street ... I believe cultural mores tell us it's OK for men to do it, but not women.

Marc, 24, Morgantown, W.Va.

I've spit into the street when there was nobody around — and no Kleenex.

Shirley, 50, Missouri

We found:

Our trajectory of research had hit a snag, and we didn't expectorate that Emily Post's great-grandson would call back, but that was before we learned he'd devoted an entire section of his New York Times-bestselling etiquette book "Essential Manners for Men" to this issue.

"What's humorous is that when I submitted that part to my editor, she said 'Why on earth do you need a section on spitting?' She was aghast ... couldn't believe there's even any discussion," said Peter Post (emilypost.com), director of the Emily Post Institute. "Then she came back and said she had to eat her words. She'd shown her husband, and he gave her a half-hour harangue about when spitting is OK and when it's not."

Turns out there are places and times for it. The athletic field, for one, or when you need to clear your throat from a cold or something and have no alternative.

"You probably don't want to land it in front of the girl you're walking with, but if you can find a place that's unobtrusive to others, it seems OK," he said.

Generally, in mixed company, swallow your enthusiasm, advised Post, who wonders whether men let fly as a result of "field of combat" historical indoctrination.

"Possibly they were involved in these things where it was the male-only bastion area [in battle or athletics], and all of a sudden, those gross forms were accepted."

Now it's evolved into unconscious ignorance.

"I don't think it's rebellion; they just don't think how it will affect people," he said.

And if you're a heavy-hitter when it comes to spitting, Post had some advice:

"Don't go to Singapore. It's against the law."

Where should he look when her boobs are ... right there?

They asked:

If you're a male client, where does your female hairstylist expect you to look when she's leaning in front of you, exposing ample cleavage?

Lee, 37, male, Fairfax, Va.

You said:

Good boys always look forward and behave when they get their hair cut. If there happens to be a pair of enormous breasts there, it's not your fault. Enjoy your haircut, and when she asks you if everything looks OK, just keep telling her your bangs need to be trimmed up more.

Joey, 25, Houston

Women earn little money and have mouths to feed. They need the tip to fill their kids' bellies. Showing cleavage = good tips = well-fed kids. To men: In order to be polite, look elsewhere and tip well. If all men didn't look, but tipped well, a woman wouldn't have to manipulate men's weakness and lower her standards.

A., 34, female, Tampa

We found:

Phone call to the spokeswoman for the National Cosmetology Association in Chicago = lots of good-natured laughs on the other end and a promise to get back quickly with a great response = no way in hell will she actually be calling back because you can keep dreamin' if you think she's getting mixed up in this one.

Therefore, it is left to Leah Ingram (leahingram.com), lifestyle expert and author of numerous books, including "The Everything Etiquette Book: A Modern-Day Guide to Good Manners" to address this most-titillating question.

She breaks it down thusly:

The stylist either a) has no idea what she is exposing, or b) is an exhibitionist.

"In the first case, pointing it out may embarrass her and affect any long-term customer relationship with her — and she may think you're harassing her," Ingram said. "In the second, if she's trying to get a rise out of a client, do you really want to put yourself in a situation where you're in the stylist chair and she's trying to turn you on? It's really a lose-lose situation if you verbalize anything."

Regarding where to cast thine eyes, Ingram advised keeping them shut.

"If she's in your face with her rack, try not to make a big issue of it. If the guy's uncomfortable — which he appears to be or he wouldn't have asked the question — he needs to find a new stylist. So often people are surprised to hear that doing nothing is the best way to handle these things. The initial instinct is to say something to try to fix it. But it doesn't always work."

In general, it's a breach of etiquette to "have a look," because wearing a revealing blouse, no matter how low-cut, does not constitute an invitation to ogle, especially in a public place such as a salon, Ingram said.

Besides, your time with a hairstylist is just that: your time. Ingram advises using it to relax or even meditate.

"That's what I do when I'm getting my hair cut. So unless the stylist needs me to refer to something, I've got my eyes closed. If this guy were to do the same, he wouldn't be faced with her bosom and tempted to say, 'Um, could you put those away?' "

With cross-dressing, is it a case of being 'so gay'?

They asked:

Why do people associate men dressing as women with homosexuality, but not vice versa? Women can wear men's clothing and nothing is thought of it, but when a man does the same with female clothing, he is stereotyped as gay or not right.

Jim W., Saginaw, Mich.

You said:

In my school, there are a lot of boys wearing girls' clothing. Mostly it's skaters or punks. I wear girl pants and find nothing wrong with it. A lot of my friends do, too. We think they're sweet. Some people have asked me, "Why do you wear those pants; are you gay?" I am straight and so are all my friends.

Logan, 15, Orange Park

A woman in jeans and a collared shirt is not going to stand out like a guy in a dress.

Kelli C., Brandon

Why would anyone want to wear women's clothing? It's uncomfortable contorting your body (high heels) or squeezing so you can barely breathe (nylons, bras). And don't get me started on skirts. Men's clothing tends to be more comfortable. Women wear women's clothing because they're expected to and it attracts men.

Avalikia, 22, female, Provo, Utah

Many people forget with fashion history that tight pants, high heels and the color pink all once belonged to men. And women were historically covered up from neck to heel, while men were the source for physical flamboyance. But the root of this "gay" association is that a woman who chooses masculine things is pursuing the "ideal," and a man who chooses feminine things is going against the ideal. A woman is choosing to be greater; a man is choosing to be lesser.

Omelio, 24, gay male, Philadelphia

We found:

We appreciate all the thoughtful replies, which mostly dealt with the cultural ramifications of average folks who occasionally don opposite-sex clothing. Stupid us, however, thought the guy was asking about full-tilt-boogie cross-dressers .

Can we just pretend he was?

Peggy Rudd's been married to one for more than 30 years and has written a number of books on the topic, including "My Husband Wears My Clothes" (PM Publishers). She says most cross-dressers aren't gay but are just getting in touch with a stronger feminine side than most men possess, one she theorizes probably originated with a greater rush of female-related hormones while they were in the womb.

"These are people who internally are more feminine with their feelings and emotions, but sexually they are men," she said.

Her husband, Mel, got on the phone to confirm that yes, a man in women's clothing is more frowned on than a woman in men's clothing.

"Men think, Why would you belittle yourself to dress like a woman?' Unfortunately many men still see women as the weaker sex ... and many people think if you dress like a man, you are upgrading your position in society."

Southern Man better keep your head...

They asked:

Movies portray Southern men as potentially dangerous. Images of evil sheriffs and psychopathic swamp dwellers come to mind whenever I'm south of Peoria. The stereotype is definitely out there. I'd love to hear from others about it.

Tom, 42, white, Wheaton, Ill.

You said:

When people hear a Southern accent, the person's IQ drops 50 points in their estimation. If you need a villain, why not pick someone who likes doing things a little slower, speaks funny and has different cultural sensitivities? It plays into the old fear that if someone is different, they are wrong and potentially evil.

Sheila, 39, white, Jacksonville

The South has long been one of the most dangerous parts of the country for anyone who isn't white. Nowhere else have I had more drunken idiots threaten me. Until your average white Southerner is more like Jimmy Carter than Zell Miller, I'll be thankful I live in a part of the South that's nothing like the rest of it.

A., male, San Antonio, Texas

There are some mean, small-minded people in the South. They are few and far between. If you want a fight, go in those little country honky-tonks. [But] as far as rednecks, I have met them in Michigan, Maine, New Hampshire, Ohio, Colorado, New York ...

Mark, Crossville, Tenn.

We found:

Don't head-butt the messenger, but it may be true that Southern males are more likely than your average Vermont office clerk to open up a can of whup-ass on somebody who crosses them.

University of Michigan social psychologist Richard Nisbett, a native Southerner and author of "Culture of Honor: The Psychology of Violence in the South" (Westview Press), says his studies show Southerners are more apt to use violence when insulted or threatened. That translates to homicide rates in small Southern communities triple that of, say, New England.

What's behind it?

The North was settled chiefly by English and German farmers, the South by herdsman from Scotland and Ireland, says Nisbett, who speculates herding people were "tough guys" whose entire livelihood was at stake if their animals weren't protected.

"You took a stance that said, 'Look at me cross-eyed and you're a dead man.' Also, Southern kids were ... taught to strike back at bullies, to make sure people don't truck with you."

That's all carried over to present-day attitudes, he said.

"The only objections [to his conclusions] come from politically correct Northerners who want to protect Southerners. But Southerners know exactly what I'm talking about. [They] regard Northerners as wimps."

"Honor violence" may be fading, however, with some evidence that Southerners overestimate the extent to which other Southerners endorse physical force, Nisbett added.

How men stomach their own big bellies

They asked:

I see a lot of men with very large stomachs. Sometimes, I see them without shirts. Men often have opinions about women's bodies. How do men with big guts feel about their own bodies?

Jazzine, 35, female, Phoenix

You said:

As a large man, I must respond. I am fully aware I need to lose weight. But there's no way in hell I'm wearing nothing but sweatshirts just because I'm less than perfect. Besides, my wife (herself a Big Black Woman) thinks I'm sexy, shirt or no shirt!

Brad, 32, Winchester, Va.

Look at most "family" sitcoms. The husband is overweight, lazy and less than intelligent. The wife is skinny, beautiful, smart, sarcastic and funny. Society tends to follow television trends. It has become OK for men to be or act dumb and be overweight. I honestly think most do not see a problem with the way they look.

Cassy, 22, Jacksonville

I have a respectable potbelly, and it's had an impact on my self-image. For a lot of my teenage years I felt my weight limited me from having romantic relationships. Lately my self-esteem has grown, and I'm of the opinion that no one should hide their bodies because they don't fit the cultural "ideal."

Andy, 19, Santa Cruz, Calif.

We found:

Beached whales in Speedos who don't give a rat's-abdomen what you think owe their attitudes to guys like John Wayne, say body image researchers. Burly dudes were the movie heroes for so many decades that it still affects men's attitudes.

Alas, men are catching up to women in body-image woes.

Beginning in the '80s with the muscled Soloflex guy and into the '90s with ripped movie stars like Keanu Reeves, Adonis-like media images were held up as the standard of the male body: slim waists, broad shoulders, rippling biceps. In the book "The Rise and Fall of Gay Culture," Daniel Harris noted that this trend began when gay men, reacting to AIDS, started valuing beefy bodies as a sign of health, and Madison Avenue and the mainstream took note.

What a shock that a Psychology Today survey showed 45 percent of men are now unhappy with their overall appearance, not far behind women at 55 percent. Sixty-three percent of the men don't like their abdomens.

Still, psychologist and Gallaudet University professor Deborah Schooler says what irks men most aren't physique issues but "real-body" issues.

Schooler published a study with L. Monique Ward of the University of Michigan that found that the more music videos and prime-time TV college-age men watched, the more they worried about things like too much body hair, excessive sweat, body odor, etc.

"These things can creep up on you unexpectedly, and you can't always manage them and they can 'betray' you in sexual situations," she said. "You focus on your shame and not your partner's needs or your sexual safety because you're less comfortable advocating for your needs. It suggests that feeling bad about your body can be unhealthy for men and women."

Barefoot, pregnant, and a turn-on for guys

They asked:

Why are some men attracted to pregnant women? My husband seems to be.

Robin, 29, Greensboro, N.C.

You said:

A pregnant woman is perceived by men as very "fragile," which reinforces a sense of vulnerability. Many men like the thought of having a sweet and beautiful woman who needs our protection.

JLM, 38, male, Kenosha, Wis.

Men are attracted to the most seemingly fertile of the opposite sex. A woman's sexuality is exaggerated in a pleasing way during pregnancy, with breasts enlarged, etc. What's not to like?

Joe P., 35, Seattle, Wash.

Men want pregnant women because dey know she ain't gonna get pregnant by them because she already pregnant. Ya dig?

S., female, Clarkesville, Md.

Men love sex, but I don't see a pregnant woman as a free lunch.

Chris, Breckenridge, Colo.

We found:

A woman can't be "a little bit" pregnant, but apparently a man can be totally turned off by, a little bit attracted to, or really juiced over, a woman in full.

Men who get off-the-charts jollies over expectant mothers may have maiesiophilia — arousal from pregnancy or childbirth, says I. David Marcus, a psychologist who specializes in sexual compulsivity at the Silicon Valley Psychotherapy Center (svpcenter.com).

"Is it a necessary condition to get aroused? Does he seek pregnant prostitutes? Does he get his wife to enact fantasies related to this? Are there secretive behaviors to get that image in his mind?"

Secretive, as in perusing the apparently numerous fetish Web sites devoted to pregnant women.

Such devotion to women with child often comes from an early childhood experience in which the person got a sexual charge in the presence of something related to pregnancy, Marcus said. Pregnancy can also symbolize security, wholesomeness and unconditional love.

What about the fertility angle? Oedipal links? The "safe sex" argument?

Those didn't retain much water for Marcus.

And just because a guy has more interest in pregnant women doesn't mean he's fixated — it's likely just one path to arousal, he said.

"This wife should express any concerns, but come from a place of curiosity. A person's arousal doesn't necessarily comment on them as a whole person ... their quality as a friend, father, empathic partner. Take it out of the closet; he may be as tormented as she is. If it's a problem, make it a common enemy, go after it as a team and preserve the good things in your marriage. In the end they may need a therapist to help talk it out."

A little blush and eyeliner with your aftershave?

They asked:

What do people think of men who wear makeup?

J., male, Clay County, Fla.

You said:

I once dated a man who wore makeup to cover blemishes and accentuate features. I didn't think he was less masculine or homosexual or anything.

Nan, 25, Albuquerque, N.M.

They should see a psychiatrist. Perhaps certain men can be excused for wearing it — such as actors, rodeo clowns and bank robbers.

Ron S., 60, Stockton, Calif.

I think it's kind of sexy. A girl can relate to wanting to look as beautiful as you can; it's nice some guys care about their appearance.

Wyn, female, Augusta, Ga.

I wore eyeliner when clubbing in L.A. (the '80s were a wacky time). I don't know why any man would wear makeup nowadays. We aren't under the same societal pressures to hide flaws as women are. As I type this, I have a zit on my cheek for all to see. That's life!

Matt, Irvine, Calif.

I kind of like a man in eyeliner. It's hot if worn right.

Rachael, 17, Fond du Lac, Wis.

We found:

This just in: The chap in the cubicle next to you may be powdering his nose. And the guy pouring the concrete slab for your new home may be laying a little foundation elsewhere as well.

U.S. sales of men's skincare products are up 13 percent, to $59 million — more than twice as fast as women's skincare sales, according to NPD Beauty, a division of market information company The NPD Group. Retail gains in men's grooming products nationwide topped 37 percent, as men catch on to the importance of looking good, according to research company Euromonitor International.

It's not just pimple cream we're talking about. Urged on by marketers, men are snapping up exfoliating facial scrub, eye gel, facial moisturizers, lip gloss (OK, lip agent), lash-styling glaze, eyeliners and nail pens, among other "men's enhancement products."

"I used to think my market was baby boomers or gay men, but it's every guy. The adolescent with acne, the college student with a presentation, the guy on his first interview," said industry pioneer Michele Probst (menaji.com), founder of Menaji cosmetics — er, skincare products — for men. "I even have brigadier generals who are clients; we've shipped stuff to them in Afghanistan."

Probst's Web site lists clients such as Barack Obama, Enrique Iglesias, Kid Rock, Tim McGraw, Tom Brokaw, Evander Holyfield and Al Gore.

Women, she said, want their men to look good. And men like the results.

"I can't tell you how many wives buy our products for their men. One lady in New Jersey, her husband is a cop and he'd been stealing her makeup, so she bought him all our stuff and put it in her drawer for him . . . now he orders it on his own."

41

New gender, new sexual orientation?

They asked:

Are men who've had a gender change attracted to men or women?

Audrey, British Columbia

You said:

My transgendered friend is "pre-op male-to-female." Although she hasn't had her operation, she presents herself as a woman. She was a heterosexual male attracted to females. Because she still prefers females, she'll be a lesbian when she makes the change.

Maria, 60, Jacksonville

I'm undergoing gender reassignment and my sex drive is zero. Some male-to-females retain their ingrained orientation, becoming lesbians, while others become what for them is heterosexual: being attracted to men. I appreciate the company of men and women. I'll let nature take its course and find my partner when the time is right.

Diana, 39, Toronto

We transsexuals are attracted to whoever we were attracted to before the sex change. If she was a gay man, she's now a straight woman. If she was a straight man, she's now a lesbian. Some people claim hormones "turned them gay" — that they were attracted to one sex and after their sex change "mysteriously" changed sexuality. But usually this means they were sexually confused to begin with.

Jack, gay, Oshkosh, Wis.

When you say "men who've had a gender change," do you mean people who transitioned from male to female or female to male?

K., 22, male, Albuquerque, N.M.

We found:

To K. in Albuquerque: We were close to having it figured out there before you chimed in, you know?

Our assignment to stop collective heads from spinning goes to Jillian Todd Weiss of JTW & Associates gender consulting and a law professor at Ramapo College of New Jersey (phobos.ramapo.edu/~jweiss).

Weiss, who was previously a male, researches workplace transgender issues. She acknowledged that for some people there may be real meaning to an old joke punch line: Yes, some straight men feel they should be women, they then become female, and then remain attracted to women — in effect, having been lesbians trapped in a man's body. (We'd been waiting to fit that line somewhere in here.)

Weiss distinguished between sex and gender. "Sex is anatomy, gender is psychology. Sex is between the legs, gender is between the ears."

She then differentiated between sexual orientation and gender identity. "Sexual orientation is about liking boys or girls; gender identity is about being boys or girls."

It's reasonable, then, to assume that the gender someone is attracted to before a sex change is the one he or she is attracted to after, she noted. That said, a sex change's biological, hormonal and sociological effects can lead some to change their orientation.

As for Weiss herself, who was married to a woman for 10 years before her operation: She's not completely sure of her orientation now, but "mostly I dig men."

Isn't reading in the bathroom a unisex thing?

They asked:

Do women not read on the toilet? Men, do you? Please say yes — and let women know about the pleasure of a really good ... read.

J., male, Orange Park

You said:

I read in the bathroom. I just finished James and the Giant Peach. Last month it was The Count of Monte Cristo. I even keep Where's Waldo and I Spy in there to keep me busy. By the way, this is also a great place to polish your toes.

Aneba, 22, female, Houston

Sorry, I'm a guy, and I don't. The entire purpose of going to the bathroom is to go to the bathroom. Maybe it's just that I grew up in a household with only one toilet.

P.R., Irvine, Calif.

Being a mom of three, sometimes the only quiet time I can get until everyone is in bed is in the bathroom. I generally keep Reader's Digest or something else on hand.

SecretMe, 40, Tacoma, Wash.

I'm a female, and I have to read something on the toilet. I'm not even picky about it. I'll read the back of a shampoo bottle, toothpaste tube, etc.

Christy, 22, Jacksonville

If you've got time to attend to anything but the matter at hand, maybe you're just not getting enough fiber in your diet.

N.J.W., 25, male, London

I sing to myself on the toilet.

Bunnie, 15, Chattanooga, Tenn.

I wonder if other women feel comfortable taking reading materials with them into the bathroom, specifically a public bathroom. Men seem to not think twice grabbing a newspaper at work and heading in.

Stacey, 30, Ellicott City, Md.

Now that I think about it, it does give you that concentration that's perfect for getting reading done.

Jamie, female, Reading, Pa.

We found:

Our mailbox overfloweth. Who better to ask about the gravity of the situation than Portable Press publisher Gordon Javna, editor in chief at the Bathroom Readers Institute in Oregon (bathroomreader.com), which has sold more than 15 million copies of its popular Uncle John's Bathroom Reader book series, produced precisely for porcelain throne perusal.

"Every survey we've seen shows that roughly two-thirds of people who can read, read in the bathroom," he said. "Since less than two-thirds of the population is male, it would be impossible for it to be only men who read in the bathroom. We get plenty of women ... who write and say they love our books."

The institute's readership is slightly skewed toward men, however, and men who read in the lavatory may spend more time in the inner sanctum than women.

However, "I don't subscribe to the theory that women are so dainty that they just get in and get out [and don't read]," Javna said firmly.

Men may also be more bold about reading in the bathroom at work, while women are more discreet about such things, perhaps preferring a more languorous approach, adds Julia Papps, production manager for the institute. That may account for the popularity of its Mom's Bathtub Reader title.

Bald-faced lie, or is hair really that prized?

They asked:

Is it true that U.S. society values men with a full, thick head of hair more than those of us who are going bald or are bald?

Andy, 36, Albany, N.Y.

You said:

Absolutely. Thick hair connotes health and youth. Also, most people's faces just aren't attractive enough to pull off the no-hair deal. Hair can often balance out or distract from features that are out of proportion, e.g., a big nose, crooked teeth, receding chin, etc.

Chris, 32, female, Rockland, Mass.

It's important what you do with your remaining hair. Don't go for a comb-over, grow it long in the back or do a "Donald Trump." It looks better if a guy just cuts his remaining hair short or shaves it completely.

A. Jacobi, female, Alexandria, Va.

Since I was 14, I have had a thing for bald men. I don't know how the United States in general views baldness, but my friends and I agree that bald = hot.

Christy, 22, Jacksonville

The media decided to portray a full head of hair on a man as the standard of beauty. If it had happened the other way around, it would be guys with all their hair who would be confused why women reject them.

Sallina H., 21, Ann Arbor, Mich.

We found:

Women's range in what they find attractive in males is much broader than what men like in women, says Michael S. Kimmel (michaelkimmel.com), a State University of New York at Stony

Brook sociologist and one of the leading researchers on men and masculinity in the world today.

"Some women like lots of body hair, some don't, some like bald men, some like beards, some like men short, some tall," said Kimmel, director of the Center for the Study of Men and Masculinities and author of books including "Manhood in America" and the best-selling "Guyland."

"Men, on the other hand, like women with big [breasts]," he said. "That's what all the research says."

Regarding baldness specifically: While women — especially those who are younger — generally find a full head of hair more attractive, there are plenty of exceptions, Kimmel said, noting that many women find naked-headers like former NBA superstar Michael Jordan "unbelievably attractive."

Indeed, a Psychology Today survey of 1,500 readers found that only 40 percent of women thought bald men were unattractive. And of women whose mates had all their hair, just 13 percent would be "very upset" and 24 percent "somewhat upset" if their hair thinned.

Much more critical to a woman than a little hair is a little class, Kimmel says.

"A bald man who presents himself elegantly and is well-dressed is better than a man with hair who dresses like a slob and has rude manners," he said. "Most women would prefer bald with a good job to a guy with hair who lives with his mother. What's attractive is a man who holds his own."

But, uh, back to that thing about men's tunnel vision. Just why do they focus on breasts?

"Because we can. Because of gender inequality in our society, we can set the standards," Kimmel says. "What gender do you think invented the thong? Women wear them because men find it attractive. Is it practical? I don't think so. We set the terms."

47

The O.U.T.L.O.U.D.
Method to Dialogue

OPEN UP: This is mostly about opening up to yourself. Why do you want to engage someone? Is it for the right reasons? The answers might help you figure out how to approach another person. A friend once told me the real reason I started Y? wasn't for me to learn more about "Buddhists in Asia or lesbians in San Francisco," but because I wanted to learn something more about myself. He was right. Acknowledging that has helped give me perspective when considering others' answers.

USE YOUR HEAD: Plan for the right question. Not all questions need to be the "wet dogs" variety. Stereotypes and clichés don't work as well as sincere attempts to talk.

TIME IT RIGHT: Create the "O.U.T.L.O.U.D. Moment". Pick your spots for provocative dialogue. Find a genuine opening rather than create a false one. It's often during those down times between all the "vital" discourse that we can most easily find a direct path to someone's point of view. If you spend enough time sitting in the cubicle next to someone of a different culture, chances are there'll come a time — over food, perhaps, or during a power outage — when the topic you've been dying to broach will wend its way naturally into the discussion.

LOCK IN ON THE TARGET: Keeping things simple can give the best chance for getting another's trust and a meaningful reply. Some of the best questions at Y?, those that prompt the most telling answers, are also often the easiest to digest. Remember, it's not about winning your point. It's what comes from the heart that counts most — and captures people's interest. Talking from the heart also means easing into things by letting someone know *why* it would help you to learn the answer to your question before you ask it.

OWN UP TO ASSUMPTIONS: One of the most refreshing and repetitive surprises of the Y? project is the difficulty in predicting how a person will respond to a question. Blacks do not think in lockstep. Nor do whites. Nor Christians or Muslims. Nor gays or straights. Be receptive to another's ideas. Wipe the slate clean and listen to the content of the message, not the color or culture of the messenger.

UNLOAD YOUR EXPECTATIONS: Many of us are thinner-skinned than we'll admit. When we get hit with an answer or comment we hadn't anticipated, our emotions can often get caught off-balance, and our egos get bruised. The solution: Expect the unexpected. You'll never be blindsided or taken aback by information that doesn't gibe with your worldview.

DIGEST THE DIALOGUE: Learning about others doesn't stop when the talking's over. Assess what you're told and how it fits with or departs from your perspectives. Recap your discussion with a third party to distill the most relevant information into its most meaningful points.

ABOUT THE AUTHOR

Phillip J. Milano is the founder of Y? The National Forum on People's Differences, the acclaimed cross-cultural dialogue project that encourages people to ask unflinching, politically incorrect questions about our differences.

Since its creation in 1998, Phillip's web site, YForum.com, has attracted millions of visitors and thousands of questions and answers. He has been featured on CBS, CNN, BET and the BBC, and in numerous newspapers, including The Washington Post, New York Times and USA Today.

He is the author of the Perigee book "I Can't Believe You Asked That!" as well as writer of the pioneering newspaper column/blog "Dare to Ask."

Mr. Milano is a 25-year newspaper veteran. He received his Master of Business Administration from Northern Illinois University and his Bachelor of Science in Journalism from Southern Illinois University.

SPEECHES AND APPEARANCES

Mr. Milano is an in-demand speaker. For bookings, contact

Contemporary Issues Agency
809 Turnberry Drive, Waunakee, WI 53597-2256
Phone: 800-843-2179
Fax: 608-849-6311
www.CIAspeakers.com
Info@CIAspeakers.com